HAL•LEONARD
INSTRUMENTAL
PLAY-ALONG

AUDIO
ACCESS
INCLUDED

PLAYBACK+
Speed • Pitch • Balance • Loop

Disney MARY POPPINS RETURNS

MUSIC BY MARC
LYRICS BY SCOTT WITTMAN

T0101640

Motion Picture Artwork TM & Copyright © 2018 Disney

Audio Arrangements by Peter Deneff

To access audio, visit:
**www.halleonard.com/mylibrary**

Enter Code
3522-0053-0951-9836

ISBN 978-1-5400-4588-1

HAL•LEONARD®

Visit Hal Leonard Online at
**www.halleonard.com**

Contact us:
**Hal Leonard**
7777 West Bluemound Road
Milwaukee, WI 53213
Email: info@halleonard.com

In Europe, contact:
**Hal Leonard Europe Limited**
42 Wigmore Street
Marylebone, London, W1U 2RN
Email: info@halleonardeurope.com

In Australia, contact:
**Hal Leonard Australia Pty. Ltd.**
4 Lentara Court
Cheltenham, Victoria, 3192 Australia
Email: info@halleonard.com.au

# CAN YOU IMAGINE THAT?

TENOR SAX

Music by MARC SHAIMAN
Lyrics by SCOTT WITTMAN and MARC SHAIMAN

# A CONVERSATION

TENOR SAX

Music by MARC SHAIMAN
Lyrics by SCOTT WITTMAN and MARC SHAIMAN

# A COVER IS NOT THE BOOK

TENOR SAX

Music by MARC SHAIMAN
Lyrics by SCOTT WITTMAN and MARC SHAIMAN

# (Underneath the)
# LOVELY LONDON SKY

TENOR SAX

Music by MARC SHAIMAN
Lyrics by SCOTT WITTMAN and MARC SHAIMAN

# NOWHERE TO GO BUT UP

TENOR SAX

Music by MARC SHAIMAN
Lyrics by SCOTT WITTMAN and MARC SHAIMAN

9

# THE PLACE WHERE LOST THINGS GO

TENOR SAX

Music by MARC SHAIMAN
Lyrics by SCOTT WITTMAN and MARC SHAIMAN

# THE ROYAL DOULTON MUSIC HALL

TENOR SAX

Music by MARC SHAIMAN
Lyrics by SCOTT WITTMAN and MARC SHAIMAN

# TRIP A LITTLE LIGHT FANTASTIC

TENOR SAX

Music by MARC SHAIMAN
Lyrics by SCOTT WITTMAN and MARC SHAIMAN

# TURNING TURTLE

TENOR SAX

Music by MARC SHAIMAN
Lyrics by SCOTT WITTMAN and MARC SHAIMAN